RAINBOW GARDEN

Written By: Anna DiGilio

All rights reserved. No part of this publication may be reproduced, distributed, or transmitted in any form or by any means, including photocopying, recording, or other electronic or mechanical methods, without the prior written permission of the publisher, except in the case of brief quotations embodied in critical reviews and certain other noncommercial uses permitted by copyright law.

For permission requests, write to the publisher:
Laprea Publishing
info@lapreapublishing.com

Website: www.GuidedReaders.com

ISBN: 978-1-63647-337-6

© 2021 Anna DiGilio

Photo Credits:
Cover, Title Page: Shutterstock; Olena Z. 3: Shutterstock; Novoselov. 4: Shutterstock; Saurabh Trehan. 5: Shutterstock; Dewi Cahyaningrum. 6: Shutterstock; Pheniti Prasomphethiran. 7: Shutterstock; Tonic Ray. 8: Shutterstock; Inmt24. 9: Shutterstock; ArinaEdemskaya. 10: Shutterstock; Eric Gevaert.

I see red!

I see yellow!

I see orange!

I see green!

I see blue!

I see purple!

I see pink!

I see a rainbow!

Read about all the colors I see in a garden.

Guided Reading Levels	
Fountas & Pinnell	A
Lexile	0L
www.GuidedReaders.com	

9 781636 473376

THE HUMAN BODY

Written By: Anna DiGilio